A fashionable HISTORY of UNDERWEAR

A FASHIONABLE HISTORY OF UNDERWEAR
was produced by

David West � **Children's Books**

7 Princeton Court
55 Felsham Road
London SW15 1AZ

Author: Helen Reynolds
Editor: Rowan Lawton
Picture Research: Carlotta Cooper
Designer: Julie Joubinaux

First published in Great Britain in 2003 by
Heinemann Library, Halley Court, Jordan Hill,
Oxford OX2 8EJ, a division of
Harcourt Education Ltd.

OXFORD MELBOURNE AUCKLAND
JOHANNESBURG BLANTYRE GABORONE
IBADAN PORTSMOUTH (NH) USA CHICAGO

Copyright © 2003 David West Children's Books

07 06 05 04 03
10 9 8 7 6 5 4 3 2 1

ISBN 0 431 18336 8 (HB)
ISBN 0 431 18344 9 (PB)

British Library Cataloguing in Publication Data

Reynolds, Helen
A fashionable history of underwear
1. Underwear - History - Juvenile literature
2. Fashion - History - Juvenile literature
I. Title II. Underwear
391.4'2'09

Printed and bound in China

PHOTO CREDITS :
Abbreviations: t-top, m-middle, b-bottom, r-right,
l-left, c-centre.

Front cover m & 10tr, r & 16l – Mary Evans
Picture Library; tl & 20bl – Karen Augusta,
www.antique-fashion.com.
Pages 3 & 7tl, 22tl, 28tl – Dover Books. 4br, 4-5,
7br, 10bl, 10-11, 15l, 22mr, 24tl & br – Karen
Augusta, www.antique-fashion.com. 5mr, 8bm, 9tr,
11m & br, 16-17, 17tr, 19br, 21tr & l, 22-23, 23tl,
tr & bl, 25br, 26br, 27l & br, 28bl, 29br – Rex
Features Ltd. 5br & 14br, 6bl, 10br, 11tl, 12bl,
13tl, bl & br, 14 both, 15tr, 18tr & bl, 20tr, 22bl,
24-25, 26tr & bl, 29tl & tr – Mary Evans Picture
Library. 6tr, 10tl, 21br, 22br, 28-29 – The Culture
Archive. 7bl – © National Trust Photographic
Library/Derrick E. Witty. 17bl – © National Trust
Photographic Library/Andreas von Einsiedel. 8bl –
© Museum of London. 12br – V&A Picture
Library. 13tr – The Kobal Collection/MGM.
15br – The Kobal Collection. 18-19 – The
Kobal Collection/Columbia. 25tr – The Kobal
Collection/RKO/Miehle, John. 23br – Hulton
Archive.

Every effort has been made to contact copyright
holders of any material reproduced in this book.
Any omissions will be rectified in subsequent
printings if notice is given to the publishers.

*An explanation of difficult words can be
found in the glossary on page 31.*

A *fashionable* HISTORY of UNDERWEAR

Heinemann
LIBRARY

Contents

BRAIES

Braies were a primitive form of pants, worn under the medieval tunic. They were held up by a braie-girdle, which was a string that threaded through the top of the garment.

CORSET

Corsets with steel insertions were worn by the end of the 19th century. Tight lacing gave the wearer the fashionable 'S' shape.

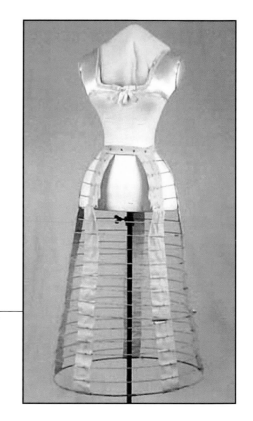

CRINOLINE

Crinolines were made of lightweight steel hoops. They were introduced to support the skirts of Victorian ladies.

From braies to fishnets

WHEN DID PEOPLE START WEARING UNDERWEAR? The first clothes, depicted on ancient wall paintings, painted pottery and mosaics, were either loincloths or simple tunics. As civilizations developed, the more prosperous began to wear additional, and finer, cloth draped or wrapped around the same simple garments. This was the beginning of underwear. By the early Middle Ages people in northern Europe were wearing what we would now describe as underwear. Braies, which developed from the loincloth, were worn by men, initially under tunics and later under breeches. The women's chemise developed out of the tunic she wore. In later centuries other layers were added, including corsets and crinolines.

LYCRA

In the late 1970s, Lycra became an important component of underwear, giving 'stretch' to make garments body-hugging and wrinkle-free – essential qualities for fishnet tights, then a popular punk fashion.

CHEMISE

The chemise, or shift, was a loose garment made of linen or cotton and worn next to the skin, from the Middle Ages until the end of the 19th century.

Why wear underwear?

TODAY WE WEAR UNDERWEAR to protect our modesty. We also wear it to help keep our bodies clean and comfortable, and to protect our outerclothes from body odours and perspiration.

Wear for all seasons

Wool and man-made thermal fibres keep us warm in winter whilst cotton and woven silk keep us cool in summer. These fabrics can be made into underwear that is designed to complement both our outerwear and taste, whether it be romantic, exotic, minimalist or simply practical.

MODESTY

The first two-pieces were worn by the Romans to exercise in, as shown in this 4th-century Roman mosaic. Romans, unlike Greeks, did not exercise naked.

CLEANLINESS

This man's fine linen undershirt (Germany, c.1515) is an outward sign of cleanliness, but in reality is worn to protect his expensive outerclothes. The woman's gown is 'slashed' on her sleeves and bodice to show her underclothes. Slashing was very common in the 16th century.

SHAPE

Stays and corsets were used to draw the body into a fashionable shape. Stiffened with whalebone, and later with steel, both garments were replaced in the 20th century by woven elastic girdles and Lycra shapers.

To protect & mould

In the past, too, underwear was worn for warmth and modesty, but also for other reasons. In many ancient civilizations, particularly the Roman Empire, washing and bathing was an important activity. However, by the Middle Ages cleanliness was not considered as important.

The magnificent materials worn at the royal courts of the Renaissance needed protection from filthy bodies. Underwear provided that protection. By the 16th century, fashionable women's underwear had yet another purpose. Through garments such as stays, corsets and hoops, underwear was used as a tool to change body shape.

WARMTH

Petticoats were often made of several layers of fabric, stitched together in a decorative design to keep the wearer warm and provide extra support for her outer skirt.
This example is a quilted petticoat (c.1840s).

COMFORT & EROTICISM

The chemise, clearly shown in this portrait of the Countess of Montagu, painted by Sir Peter Lely (1616–80), protects the skin from the expensive yet rough fabric of the gown, but also conveys an erotic mood, as the painter intended.

The underpinning of fashion

ALTHOUGH UNDERWEAR HAS ITS OWN FASHIONABLE HISTORY, *it plays a vital role in supporting the rest of fashion.*

Men's shapely underwear

Shape-altering devices have been used mainly by women, but men have not always been averse to some enhancement. For example, the 16th-century padded codpiece, a pouch that covered the male genitalia, was very prominent. Artificial calves created some 18th-century dandies' shapely legs, while many 19th-century gentlemen resorted to a pair of stays (see page 10).

SHAPING MEN'S BODIES

At the beginning of the 19th century the cut of men's frock coats and breeches allowed little room for ease and highlighted any excess weight. This led many a fashionable dandy to resort to the methods illustrated. Nowadays the figure-conscious man wears well-fitting, cotton-lycra underwear, follows a low-fat diet and goes to the gym.

S-SHAPE UNDERWEAR

The 'S' bend was the shape of fashionable women at the turn of the 20th century. It was immortalized by the artist Charles Gibson (1867–1944) and his model, the Gibson girl. The corset supported the bust and thrust it forward. This created the ample Edwardian bosom, while tight lacing drew in the waist and hips.

Corsets like this one could only be worn by women who needed to do little bending or lifting, as rigid bones were inserted in the seams.

Drawers or knickers were now long and narrow.

Until 1920, stockings were made of wool or cotton lisle. Expensive, they would be repaired if they tore.

The function of underwear

After World War II (1939–45), at the time of designing his New Look which threw off the constraints of the war, the fashion designer Christian Dior (1905–57) wrote that *'without foundations there can be no fashionable dress'*. Part of the function of underwear was, and still is today, to mould the figure into the fashionable shape of the time. Throughout history the fashionable silhouette could never have been achieved without the corresponding underwear.

Women today

Today most women seek comfortable underwear for their busy lifestyles and have abandoned the corset, but the bra, which is a shape enhancer, remains as popular as ever.

Corsets like this one were made to create the popular wasp-waist effect.

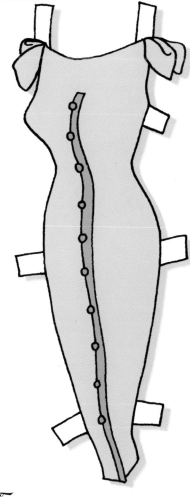

Suspenders were attached to the corset to hold up the stockings.

Stockings, or nylons as they were known, were now 'fully fashioned', which eliminated unsightly wrinkles around the ankles.

Fifties waspie underwear

The 1950s' corselette included elastic and the new nylon in its construction, which flattened the figure rather than drawing it in, making it relatively more comfortable to wear. The salmon pink colour was fashionable.

Corsets & stays

APART FROM THE BRIEF PERIODS IN HISTORY *when the fashionable waist has been high, low or even obliterated, women's fashions have centred on the waist, resulting in women seeking undergarments that compress the waist and, on occasions, the chest and hips by means of a stay, corset or girdle.*

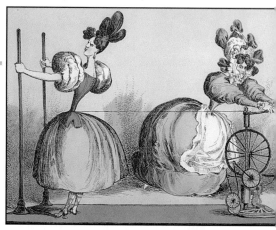

Getting it on

Very tight corsets were the preserve of the rich who could afford ladies' maids to lace them. However, pulleys such as this were also patented and sold.

Minoan

This Minoan statue, wearing a corset-like garment, dates from around 2000 BCE.

Cane, whalebone & steel

In 15th-century Europe, when bodices became shaped and skirts widened, women were wearing a 'pair of bodies' or 'stays', initially of stiffened cloth, then seamed and shaped with cane and whalebone to provide rigidity. By the 16th century stays had been replaced by the more rigid corset. During the 19th century, tight lacing became a subject of controversy with women's rights groups, advocating its abandonment.

Stays

These stays (1876) were heavy linen or cotton, stiffened with whalebone and were worn over a chemise.

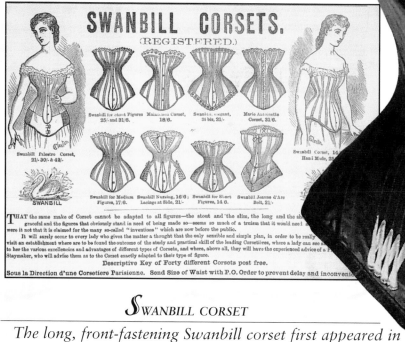

SWANBILL CORSETS.
(REGISTERED.)

Swanbill for stout Figures 25/- and 31/6. Maintenon Corset, 18/6. Swanbill, elegant, 34 bis, 21/-. Marie Antoinette Corset, 31/6.

Swanbill Palestro Corset, 21/- 30/- & 42/-.

Swanbill for Medium Figures, 17/6. Swanbill Nursing, 16/6, Lacings at Side, 21/-. Swanbill for Short Figures, 14/6. Swanbill Jeanne d'Arc Belt, 21/-.

Swanbill Corset, 14/- Hand Made, 25/-

THAT the same make of Corset cannot be adapted to all figures—the stout and the slim, the long and the short graceful and the figures that obviously stand in need of being made so—seems so much of a truism that it would need were it not that it is claimed for the many so-called "inventions" which are now before the public.

It will surely occur to every lady who gives the matter a thought that the only sensible and simple plan, in order to be really visit an establishment where are to be found the outcome of the study and practical skill of the leading Corsetières, where a lady can see a to her the various excellencies and advantages of different types of Corsets, and where, above all, they will have the experienced advice of a P Staymaker, who will advise them as to the Corset exactly adapted to their type of figure.

Descriptive Key of Forty different Corsets post free.

Sous la Direction d'une Corsetiere Parisienne. Send Size of Waist with P.O. Order to prevent delay and inconveni

Swanbill corset

The long, front-fastening Swanbill corset first appeared in the 1870s. It had bust supports and widened at the hips giving it its characteristic pear shape. The Swanbill corset was often advertised as being particularly suitable for the 'stout figure'.

BODY DAMAGE

In the 19th century many women wore corsets during adolescence and pregnancy. Both the medical profession and women's groups campaigned against tight lacing.

Roll-ons & girdles

The dress reform movement spread rapidly, but the fashionable lady continued to lace, and corsets became more restrictive to encompass the hips. But early in the 20th century, women's lives, and technology, changed. Designers, including Paul Poiret (1879–1944) and Madeleine Vionnet (1876–1975), pioneered looser styles, worn with more comfortable roll-ons and girdles that flattened the waist with elastic materials, instead of laces.

DIOR WASPIES

In 1947 some corsets briefly became more restrictive as they gave shape to Dior's hourglass New Look. Some models of the waspie, as it was known, had laced backs but most also had elastic insets, making them much more comfortable than their Victorian predecessors.

A BRIGHTLY-DYED CORSET

Non washable, corsets like this late 19th-century one had to be worn over a chemise or camisole.

LASTEX 40S STYLE

Corselettes were made of Lastex and satin nylon. Woven elastic and nylon made corsets more comfortable, washable and glamorous.

Bum-rolls, bustles, crinolines,

WIDE SKIRTS NEED SUPPORT. *The farthingale, bum-roll, pannier, crinoline and bustle provided that support. In the European courts of the 16th century, social standing was very dependent on how lavishly one dressed.*

From farthingales to panniers

The farthingale, a petticoat with hoops of cane, was a device to display fashionable heavy silk brocades and damasks to their full advantage. Farthingales were a highly impractical court fashion, so many women resorted to a bum-roll – a sausage of stuffed material that tied at the front. In the 1620s, when fashionable silks became lighter, the farthingale disappeared. The hoop, however, reappeared in the 18th century. These hooped petticoats were made of cane, whalebone or wire and were bell-shaped. This shape was later flattened at the back and front to become two panniers extending out at each hip.

BUM-ROLLS

The stuffed bum-roll was tied beneath the skirt (c.1600).

PANNIERS

Panniers worn at court were huge, and extended to a width of 1.5 metres. Some were even hinged so the wearer could negotiate small spaces more easily.

FARTHINGALE LOOK

The Spanish farthingale (left) was replaced by the wider French farthingale when, later in her reign, Queen Elizabeth I (1533–1603) opposed any Spanish influence on her court dress.

farthingales & hoops

CRINOLINE FACTORY

Crinolines were mass-produced in factories where up to a 1,000 women made 4,000 of them in a single day.

HOOPS

Elizabeth Taylor wore a crinoline in the film Raintree County (1957). The hoops can be seen here clearly.

THE NEW

Canfields

BUSTLE
FOR THE MILLION

By Royal Letters Patent, No. 6.043.

So arranged with a spring as to fold up when wearer is sitting or lying down, the Bustle resuming its proper position upon rising.

Size can be altered by means of an adjustable cord.

Light, cool, easy to wear, never gets out of order, and is the correct Parisian shape. Best Bustle to fit a dress over. The only Bustle ever made to fit any lady and every dress.

Depth, including band, 11 in

OF ALL DRAPERS AND LADIES' OUTFITTERS THROUGHOUT THE KINGDOM.

Price 2s. 6d.

By post 3d. extra. Send Stamps or Postal Order.

WHOLESALE ONLY

STAPLEY and SMITH,
LONDON WALL, LONDON, E.C.

BUSTLES

By 1865 the crinoline had flattened in front to form the crinolette, and later the bustle, as shown here (c.1887).

The crinoline

The crinoline was introduced in the mid-19th century when the new fashionable wide skirts were weighed down by layers of petticoats. The French Empress, Eugénie (1826–1920) helped to promote the style. However, unlike the hoops of the previous century, this crinoline was mass-produced and had lightweight steel hoops. It was cheap enough for large numbers of women to adopt the fashion.

TOO WIDE

It was very easy to mock crinolines. Cartoonists of the time did so frequently, as in this example from 1855.

Chemise, vest & petticoat

EARLY WOMEN'S UNDERWEAR *dates back to ancient times. These chemises, vests and petticoats developed into combination garments before becoming functional separates in the 20th century.*

The tunic

The chemise, or shift, was a simple tunic made of two rectangles of material. It remained almost unchanged from the Greek and Roman empires to the 20th century, when the tunic shape was adapted by designers such as Fortuny (1871–1949), Chanel (1883–1971) and Balenciaga (1895–1972). From the early medieval period to the 19th century, the simple chemise was the undergarment that women wore next to the skin, and over which would be added stays, corsets and waist petticoats.

ANCIENT VESTS

The ancient Romans wore simple tunics next to their skin. The more affluent draped and layered a toga over them. In medieval Europe the tunic evolved into the women's chemise and man's shirt.

CHILDREN'S UNDERWEAR

Children did not have their own styles of underwear until the 20th century. Before that they often wore miniature versions of their parents' clothes.

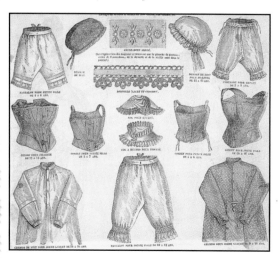

CHEMISE

The chemise, or shift, was a woman's shirt, or loose-fitting dress worn as underclothes up until the late 1800s. This garment was the forerunner of modern underwear.

TEDDY

Pastel-coloured teddies became popular in the 1920s. Teddies were derived from chemises and drawers, and perfectly complemented the slender, dropped-waist fashions of the period.

Sensible underwear

The chemise finally lost favour at the end of the 19th century, as a new plethora of elaborately trimmed and embroidered 'frilly and frothy' undergarments became fashionable. These included combination garments like the cami-knicker, the cami-bocker and teddies. In contrast to these decorative undergarments, the same period saw the rise of functional, 'sensible' underwear. This coincided with the popularity of outdoor leisure activities – including riding the latest invention, the bicycle. Fabrics for this utilitarian underwear included wool (which Dr Gustav Jaeger claimed rid the body of noxious exhalations), aertex and viyella – a soft blend of wool and cotton that first appeared in 1891.

PETTICOAT

In spite of Victorian and Edwardian modesty, petticoats were exposed in images on seaside amusement piers, and in music halls by performing chorus girls.

T-SHIRT

Cotton, knitted T-shirts were first issued to US servicemen to wear under their uniforms in World War I (1914–18). They were later worn by labourers, but also became a cult fashion for male teenagers of the 1950s, when they were worn by film stars, including Marlon Brando (right) and James Dean.

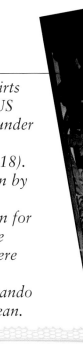

Drawers, knickers & pants

UNTIL THE BEGINNING OF THE 19TH CENTURY respectable women wore nothing under their chemise. The equivalent of modern knickers were first worn in the 1800s, when women's fashions followed classical lines. The high-waisted and narrow gowns allowed little room for voluminous petticoats, so pantaloons and drawers were borrowed from the man's wardrobe in the interest of modesty.

Drawers

During the reign of Queen Victoria (1837–1901) wide skirts and multiple layers became fashionable again, but drawers remained. They were now established in women's wardrobes and suited the outwardly chaste and prudish Victorian society. Drawers were predominately white cotton, loose and open-crotched, with each leg attached to a wide waistband. But by the mid-1850s, drawers were increasingly heavily trimmed with lace, and were also made out of wool, flannel and silk.

PANTALOONS

These long pantaloons of the 1920s were edged with white lace. This style is reminiscent of a Victorian lady's drawers.

The British Utility scheme of 1940 urged women to buy durable wear and offered summer and winter styles. Soldiers called them 'passion killers'!

*K*nickers

By the end of the 19th century the gusset seam on drawers had closed, and the term knickers had come into use. Knickers were still held up with ties, wide waistbands and buttons. Some ingenious devices were used to avoid pulling them up and down, including a back flap known as a 'trap door'. In the 1920s woven elastic was incorporated into the waistband and rayon was used. Shorter, frillier styles became fashionable.

Y-FRONTS FOR WOMEN!

Today many designers make ranges of unisex underwear, although it is cut differently for each sex. Above is a Calvin Klein Y-front pants and vest set.

*C*AMI-KNICKERS

These 1940s salmon pink cami-knickers and cream lace bra and knickers set were made of nylon, which was considered very luxurious at the time.

*T*HE THONG

Thongs became popular in the 1990s, as a way of avoiding a knicker line under body-hugging clothes.

Men's pants, Y-fronts & boxers

MUNLIKE MANY ITEMS of *women's* undergarments, men's underwear is usually mainly practical and pants are no exception. In recent times pants have been styled to the contours of the body, using sturdy fabrics and utilizing the latest construction techniques.

Braies

Braies were a single piece of fabric, drawn up between the legs and threaded on a string at the waist.

Early drawers

In Medieval Europe braies were worn under male tunics. Braies, later known as drawers, were the forerunner of modern pants, with one big difference – no crotch seam. By the end of the 18th century, drawers had narrowed to avoid appearing bulky under tight breeches.

Loose underwear

Worn by generations of Americans, B.V.D.'s loose-fitting underwear was ideal for warm weather.

Ventilated underwear

By the 20th century the Industrial Revolution was well advanced, and men's underpants, previously sewn in the home, were produced in factories in increasing volumes.

Long johns

Long johns first appeared in the 19th century. Burt Lancaster wore them in The Gunslingers *movie, set in 1917.*

From drawers to pants

During the 19th century drawers were long or knee-length. Buttons were added, and by the end of the century the crotch had closed, apart from a front flap. After World War I, the styling of men's pants was refined to coincide with the advent of the motor car, jazz and the new age of modernity. Elastic began to be used in waistbands, although it was largely unavailable during World War II. Advertisements of the time started to show photographs of well-exercised, suntanned men in figure-hugging styles.

THERMALS

Thermal underwear, styled after the long johns of old, was promoted as undies for all in the 1980s. Made in practical, natural fibres such as silk or cotton, they provide maximum warmth, but have never achieved real popularity.

Y-FRONTS

In the 1930s the American men's underwear firm, Coppers, introduced skimpy Y-front pants known as Jockey briefs. This style is still popular today.

BOXERS

Boxer shorts were only made possible when elastic could be incorporated into waistbands. First worn in the boxing ring, they were later adapted for underwear.

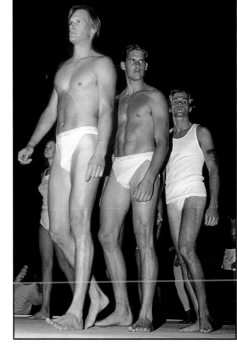

The bra

ALTHOUGH BREAST BANDS ARE ILLUSTRATED on some ancient mosaics, and 'bust improvers' were advertised in magazines in the last quarter of the 19th century, the brassiere is essentially a 20th-century innovation. First patented in America in 1914 by Mary Phelps Jacob for Caress Crosby, the brassiere was originally designed to flatten the bust.

l'élégance madame commence par...

DéWé

The jazz-age brassiere

Following World War I, the tight-laced corset was totally abandoned and a type of brassiere was introduced that all but obliterated the bust. The brassiere proved to be a comfortable foundation for the unstructured, tubular dresses of the jazz age, designed for the emancipated woman. As the 1920s progressed, the brassiere began to incorporate woven elastic straps and back. By the 1930s the bust and waistline had become fashionable again and corsetry companies revived their flagging sales by revamping brassieres as structured and boned garments.

EARLY BRAS

The brassiere helped to give 1920s women the tubular look that was the prerequisite for the flapper dress of the jazz age.

Gossard first produced the Wonderbra in 1969. It became a bestseller and has been widely copied. The aim of the Wonderbra is to push the bust up in order to provide maximum cleavage.

This US advertising campaign of 1955, for the Maidenform company, was very important in popularizing the bra as a new fashion item in underwear.

The modern bra

The bra, as it was now called, began to incorporate padding and was at its most exaggerated during the 1950s, when fashion required a prominent bust. As fashion moved towards a younger look in the 1960s, the padding was drastically reduced to give a natural, youthful shape. Lycra was introduced by bra manufacturers in the late 1970s. Ironically, since it was originally a liberating garment, women's liberation groups chose the bra as the symbol of female oppression and advocated bra burning. However, today the bra remains as popular as ever and an essential part of women's wardrobes.

MISSILE SILHOUETTE

The sweater, or missile, bra was worn by Hollywood film stars like Jane Russell and Jayne Mansfield (above). It created an exaggerated, high, pointed bosom. This would be impossible to achieve naturally.

Socks & stockings

EARLY STOCKINGS, OR HOSE, *were simple cloth bandages wound round the leg. Later stockings were cut from woven material, either on the grain of the fabric or diagonally on the bias, which gave a better fit. In many of the European courts of the 16th century there are references to fine knitted silk stockings.*

Men in tights

Men's tights were called hose and were cut to fit the shape of the leg. They were worn in a variety of lengths.

Socks & clocks

The stocking frame machine was invented around 1600 by William Lee. However, this machine had to undergo a number of improvements before it became real competition for hand knitted socks. Although the majority of socks produced were plain, coarse knitted wool, very fine silk socks were worn by the wealthy. Embroidered 'clocks' sometimes decorated the triangular gore in the ankle seams, which worked well with men's knee breeches.

Early stockings

Colourful gore clock stockings (c.1720–40) were worn by both sexes. The designs often reached to mid calf.

Men's suspenders

During World War II in Britain, the majority of available elastic was used by the armed forces. Socks were manufactured without elastic tops, forcing men to resort to old-fashioned suspenders.

Natural fibres

Everyday Victorian stockings were made of wool or cotton lisle. Unlike today, stockings were relatively expensive. Women, or their sewing maids, would regularly darn holes in them.

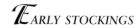

Rayon

Rayon stockings first appeared in the 1920s as an alternative to silk. They were incredibly shiny and gave ordinary women their first chance to wear fine stockings.

$\mathcal{T}$IGHTS

White lacy tights were sold through high street outlets. Although the first tights were very expensive, they were readily bought in all colours and deniers (thicknesses) by teenagers, to wear under miniskirts.

$\mathcal{F}$ISHNETS

Fishnet refers to the net pattern on some tights and stockings. They have recently been revived as part of mainstream fashion.

$\mathcal{K}$EEPING THEM UP

Silk stockings had no elasticity to keep them up. So suspenders attached to a suspender belt, or to underwear, were used to avoid unsightly wrinkles.

$\mathcal{T}$he modern stocking

In the late 1870s a number of suspender belt devices, to hold up women's stockings, were patented. As skirts became shorter in the 1920s, more emphasis was placed on stockings. Rayon was used as a cheaper alternative to silk and heavy cotton lisle. Fully-fashioned stockings appeared in the 1920s, eliminating wrinkles. After World War II, when shortages forced many women to wear ankle socks, 'nylons' became widely available in fine deniers. In the late 1950s pantie-hose, or tights, became available. Sales of tights soared as designers like Mary Quant (*b*.1934) made miniskirts fashionable in the 1960s.

$\mathcal{N}$YLON MANUFACTURE

Nylon stockings were mass-produced from the 1940s, making them accessible to most women.

Nightshirts & fine lingerie

UNTIL THE 19TH CENTURY, *night clothes were the preserve of the better-off. For the majority of the population the chemise and shirt worn next to the skin doubled as night attire. According to accounts of Henry VIII's wardrobe he wore a special gown at night, as did his daughters, Queen Mary (1516–58) and Queen Elizabeth (1533–1603).*

Nightshirts & shifts

These garments of 1860 were made in linen or cotton muslin, with simple embroidery.

Nightwear

not underwear

During Queen Victoria's reign, separate nightwear was more widely worn. Women's white nightdresses were voluminous affairs with high collars, yokes and deep cuffs. By the late 19th century pyjamas were steadily replacing the man's night shirt. The wealthy often had their initials, or ciphers, embroidered on nightwear. At the turn of the 20th century the term lingerie was being used. Opulent, and often very beautiful, but totally impractical, boudoir gowns and negligees were worn by wealthy ladies at home, under loosened corsets.

Nightdress

Sumptuous nightdresses in sheer silk, such as this halterneck model, were popular in the 1930s, with those who could afford them!

VIYELLA NIGHTWEAR

Viyella is made of 55% wool and 45% cotton, so has the warmth of wool and the absorbency of cotton. Viyella also has superb draping qualities which made it very popular for use in loose garments gathered on a yoke.

ELLA
REGᴰ

& NIGHT
WEAR

T SHRINK

War Department

Fine lingerie

Until the beginning of the 20th century fine lingerie (and other underwear) was sold by the dress designer Lucile (1863–1935) at her salons in London, Paris, New York and Chicago. Her fine, gossamer lingerie, in pastel colours, was extremely expensive and considered rather risqué and daring. However, it was much prized and sold well to actresses, music hall artists, young brides and mature ladies. Lucile's creations were widely imitated by manufacturers of cheaper lingerie. In the 1920s rayon made frilly nightwear even cheaper, and by the 1950s nylon became the typical material of mass-produced negligees. But alongside these frilly creations, the market for practical nightwear has continued to thrive.

PYJAMAS

In the 1920s women adopted this man's garment turning it into leisure and beachwear. By the 1950s it had become the typical housewife's cosy night attire.

BABY DOLL

Nylon Baby doll sleepwear consisted of a hip-length nightie with matching knickers. Popular with teenage girls of the 1960s, Baby dolls were first introduced in the late 1950s and were popularized by the film of the same name.

Underwear as outerwear

UNDERWEAR IS THE PRIVATE CLOTHES WE WEAR *'under'* our public clothes. The Victorians, for all their outward prudishness, were largely responsible for putting the frills and fripperies into what were otherwise quite plain garments. It is at this period that some underwear came to be regarded as erotic and sensual. It was also the age when the 'peep show' was introduced and women would be displayed in various states of undress.

Bloomerism

In 1851, Amelia Bloomer (1818–94) and other ladies of Seneca Falls in New York State, devised a practical, short dress. The dress exposed Turkish-style pantaloons. It was highly ridiculed.

Versatile underwear

The Greeks and Romans regarded under and outerwear as totally interchangeable. Throughout history this idea has persisted, and underwear has often been exposed. In Tudor times the overskirt was left open in the front to reveal a flamboyant underskirt. In the 16th century a type of corset was sometimes worn over the chemise, with a skirt, on informal occasions. Today too, some fashions have been inspired by underwear. Camisole tops and frilly skirts are ever-popular while skateboarders and other fashionable young people wear trousers that expose their boxer shorts.

Tudor underskirt

In the 16th century the underskirt, or top petticoat, was often designed to be seen and so was made out of lavish material.

Laura Ashley petticoats

Laura Ashley dresses became very fashionable in the 1970s. Many of her styles exposed frilly petticoats.

Vivienne Westwood

Vivienne Westwood (b.1941) designed corsets and crinolines as outerwear for the 1992 London Fashion Week. She claimed these corsets were not restrictive, but sexy! Westwood is notorious for creating garments that shock. Her innovative takes on fashions from the past, combined with exquisite tailoring, keep her in the forefront of world fashion in the 21st century.

Madonna

The pop singer and actress Madonna popularized the wearing of underwear as outerwear. She wore this bustier, with its cone-shaped bra and suspenders, on her tour in the early 1990s. It was made for her by Jean-Paul Gaultier.

Wash 'n' wear

BEFORE THE INTRODUCTION OF THE SEWING MACHINE *and mass-produced, machine-made clothes in the 19th century, underwear was* expensive in relation to average incomes. It was not unusual for people to own just one or two sets of underclothes. As factories produced cheaper underwear, working people changed their's more regularly.

Not to wash

The earliest underwear was made of linen and wool. In the 19th century cotton and silk was used. Chemises and drawers were washable, but corsets and crinolines contained horsehair stuffing, whalebone, cane, wood, leather and steel, making them almost impossible to clean.

Metal gear

Corsets were feminine, pretty and popular for centuries but, manufactured from water-shy materials, they were not very practical garments.

Machine-made

Children used to work in clothing factories from a very young age, producing underwear garments, such as stockings.

By the 1930s, elastic 'Lastex' yarns were woven into fabrics, making girdles softer, flexible and more comfortable. Aertex, a cotton, cellular fabric that trapped air in holes in the weave, was first introduced in the late 1880s.

*T*o wash

By 1920 washable rayon and woven elastic had replaced the absurdly impractical materials. In the 1940s nylon was introduced into the commercial market with polyester following soon after. Finally, Lycra was incorporated into fabrics in the 1970s. Mixed with other fibres, Lycra gives fabric oustanding stretch and recovery properties, making today's underwear easy-care, body-hugging, absorbent – and clean!

*L*YCRA

Du Pont first introduced Lycra into the USA in 1958. Lycra is used in much of today's underwear, including the cotton garments shown here, by Sloggi. Lycra is always mixed with another fibre, either by being covered with it (1), forced through an air jet with the other fibre, coating it in a lacework of strands (2) or twisted with it as it is spun (3).

1

Thread

Lycra

2

3

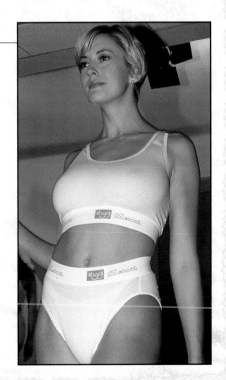

Timeline

The ancient world
Underwear and outerwear were interchangeable in this period. Extra layers of clothing were added, or removed, according to the weather. As societies developed, the layers next to the skin, the loincloth and tunic, became covered. Undergarments had arrived to stay.

The Middle Ages
During this time undergarments were plain and simple. The tunic had developed into the women's 'T'-shaped smock, or chemise. This garment was to remain part of women's underwear until the 19th century. Men wore simple shirts and primitive pants called braies, which were a garment very similar to the loincloth.

16th century
The 16th century saw differences in underwear between different ranks of society. Women used underwear to change their body shape. The stiffened bodice, or 'body', incorporated wood, whalebone and occasionally iron bands to shape the fashionable, elongated bodice and small waist. In this century the farthingale was devised. This hooped structure held out skirts and was worn by ladies of high rank. Bum-rolls provided an alternative to this highly impractical fashion. Men's white shirts were displayed through slashes in the doublet.

17th century
Waist petticoats had replaced farthingales, as fashionable material became lighter. The boned 'stay' was an early form of the corset and was an important part of women's wardrobes. Many working women often resorted to unboned models, made of thick leather. Men continued to wear white shirts. The shirts of the nobility were made of fine linen with embroidery or lace around the neck and cuffs. Drawers had now replaced braies.

18th century
Fashionable women's underwear in this century was dominated by the hoop petticoat. At the beginning of the century it was bell-shaped, but around the middle of the 1700s it had flattened and become a 'pair of panniers', resting on each side of the hips and reaching fantastic widths. Towards the end of the century hoops ceased to be worn, as waistlines rose to just below the bust. Stays became shorter and less restrictive. Men continued to wear loose shirts and drawers. Some dandies resorted to artificial calves and stays.

19th century
At the beginning of this century women started to wear drawers under transparent muslin dresses. Cotton drawers continued to be worn under steel-framed crinolines, from the 1850s. Crinolines, manufactured in large quantities, were slowly flattened in front and renamed the crinolette. This garment then developed into the bustle. By the end of the century fashionable women were wearing restrictive corsets, which ended on the hip. This corset enabled women to be drawn into the fashionable 'S' shape. In the 1880s Dr Jaeger introduced sanitary wool underwear, made into the new men's long johns and vests.

20th century & beyond
Fashionable lingerie and underwear was now very feminine and often made in silk. Closed-gusset knickers had replaced drawers. Cami-knickers were very popular in the 1920s, as underwear needed to be unobtrusive under slimline, drop-waisted, 'flapper' dresses. The brassiere began to be widely worn in the 1920s. Girdles with elastic insets were replacing the corset. Rayon and nylon were popular new underwear fabrics. In the 1920s men began to wear figure-hugging trunks and the inclusion of elastic into waistbands paved the way for Y-fronts and boxers. Lycra is now the must-have component of modern stretch underwear for men and women in the 21st century.

Glossary

Breeches

A term used to describe a variety of male garments such as 15th-century primitive tights. By the end of the 16th century the term breeches described male trousers that ended at the knee.

Cami-bockers

Similar to cami-knickers, cami-bockers had gathered legs and a back flap opening that fastened at the back of the waist. They were popular in the 1910s and 1920s.

Denier

The thickness of the yarn in stockings or tights. The higher the number denier, the thicker the yarn. For example 40 denier tights are thicker than 10 denier tights.

Girdle

A flexible type of corset with elastic panelling, that extends over the hips. A girdle was also a sash worn around the waist, from which various objects, such as household keys, could be hung.

Lisle

A fibre which is spun from tightly twisted cotton, or linen, and used to make hardwearing stockings.

Negligee

A light loose robe, like a dressing gown, that was first worn informally at home in the late 19th century. Negligees were frilly and were usually trimmed with lace. Since the 20th century the simpler dressing gown has largely replaced the negligee.

Pannier

A hooped petticoat which looks similar to the 19th-century crinoline, panniers were worn in the 18th century to support the gowns of aristocratic women.

Rayon

Man-made cellulose fibre derived from wood pulp, rayon was first spun into fabric in 1884 and developed commercially in the 20th century.

Roll-on

A tightly-elasticated girdle without a fastening that was literally 'rolled' on to the body. Roll-ons were popular in the 1950s and 1960s.

Teddy

The American term for the cami-knicker, the modern version being loose French-style knickers attached to a camisole top.

Thong

Modern knickers with a single cord at the back to ensure that no knicker line is visible under figure-hugging clothes.